Friend Grief and Men: Defying Stereotypes

VICTORIA NOE

Copyright © 2016 Victoria Noe

All rights reserved. This book or any portion thereof may not be reproduced or used in any manner whatsoever without the express written permission of the publisher except for the use of brief quotations in a book review.

This book is not intended as a substitute for therapeutic or medical advice. The reader should regularly consult a medical professional in matters relating to his/her health and particularly with respect to any symptoms that may require diagnosis or medical attention.

For a list of grief support resources: www.VictoriaNoe.com

Printed in the United States of America

First Printing, 2016

ISBN
   978-0-9903081-6-4 paperback
   978-0-9903081-7-1 epub
   978-0-9903081-8-8 mobi

King Company Publishing – Chicago, IL 60618

www.VictoriaNoe.com

The Clarity and Confusion of Grief, reprinted by permission, Jeff Goins.

Disenfranchised Grief: New Directions, Challenges and Strategies for Practice, reprinted by permission, Kenneth J. Doka, Ed.

When Men Grieve: Why Men Grieve Differently and How You Can Help Them, reprinted by permission, Elizabeth Levang, Ph.D., Fairview Press.

Brian Piccolo: A Short Season, reprinted by permission, Jeannie Morris, Rowman & Littlefield Publishers.

Rebel Friendships: "Outsider" Networks and Social Movements, reprinted by permission, Benjamin Heim Shepard.

The AIDS Generation: Stories of Survival and Resilience, reprinted by permission, Oxford University Press.

Table of Contents

Introduction 1

Do Men Really Grieve Differently?........................... 5

"It Changed My Life Forever." 13

More than Sports.. 21

How Deep Are Their Friendships? 27

"All My Friends Are Dead." 35

"Ask God to Love Him, Too." 41

Veterans of Two Very Different Wars 47

A Life Dedicated to Their Friends 59

Final Thoughts... 65

Acknowledgements 71

References.. 73

Resources... 75

Dedication

My father's friends were loud, sometimes profane, argumentative and fun. I was born in the 50's so I still call them "mister". I've never felt comfortable calling them by their first names.

You know how it is with the generation older than you: they've always been around and you assume they always will be. But, of course, that's not true.

In 2005, Daddy was the first in his group to die, a few weeks before his seventy-seventh birthday. I don't know how much they talked about his illness when I wasn't around. I do know that as shocked and worried as they were about his prognosis, they did not abandon him.

In some ways, they did what a lot of men do when something bad is happening: they ignored it. They were still loud, profane, argumentative and fun. That had to be a comfort to my father, even as he also pretended everything was fine.

And when it mattered, they showed up – one within the hour – after we finally called in hospice care. Another – the loudest, funniest, most profane and argumentative – took one look at Daddy in his hospital bed in the living room and bolted for the front porch to fall apart.

They came to the wake and served as pallbearers. They picked up my mother for occasional group lunches. They took her out to breakfast.

The group is smaller now, and in a few years it will be gone completely. My father was a good friend to them and that love was returned, though not perhaps in ways that were obvious. I'll always be grateful for their love.

This book is dedicated to my father and his friends: Mr. Guthrie, Mr. D'Angelo, Mr. Salmieri, Mr. Coughlin and Jake Taylor (the exception to the "mister" rule because he's almost always referred to by his full name). Someday they'll all be together again, to tease and joke and solve the problems of the world while drinking scotch and listening to Sinatra.

And that will be a very good day.

Introduction

Mea culpa.
Mea culpa.
Mea maxima culpa.

When I started writing the *Friend Grief* books, I felt uniquely unqualified to interview people about their experiences grieving the death of a friend. I'm not a therapist or counselor. I have a master's degree in speech and dramatic art, not psychology. Why would anyone talk to me?

As it turned out, it wasn't hard to find people who wanted to talk about this particular kind of grief. I quickly realized why. They talked to me because I *wasn't* a therapist or counselor. I wasn't there to diagnose them. I was only there to listen. I've listened to a lot of people eager to share their stories about friends they loved and missed. One thing, however, took me completely by surprise.

Men.

I began this journey assuming that getting men to talk would be difficult, if not impossible. After all, men don't talk about their feelings, do they? Men's friendships aren't as deep as women's, are they?

I was wrong. So wrong.

The men I interviewed needed little encouragement to tell me about their friends. Two came to me, wanting to tell their stories. I met some in public places: a sports bar, a neighborhood diner, a trendy restaurant. I came armed with questions to spark discussion that proved unnecessary. They wanted to talk. They needed to talk because for most it was the first time they would share their stories.

At first the conversations felt awkward. All of the men warmed quickly, recounting the history of their friendships and their struggles with grief. A few cried, which upset me. It was not my intent to make them cry. But eventually I realized it was a compliment: they felt comfortable enough with me to let their guard down, even in a public place.

I wasn't there to tell them how they should feel or behave. I was just there to listen. It's why I tell people who don't know what to say to a grieving person, "Just listen".

Some of the men followed up with emails including more information about their friend or a story they'd forgotten to tell me. One asked me to come back to talk more. Every one of them, I realize now, was smiling and happy when we finished. I assumed they were happy our time was up. But it became clear as I interviewed more and more men that they were happy to have shared the most important friendships of their lives. For a little while, as we sat in that bar or diner or office, their friend was alive. The stories told, the tears shed, reminded them of the impact of their friendship.

I saved a lot of their interviews because I decided that men deserved their own book. Some of these could've fit into previous books in the series. A couple of the men appeared in those books, too. But by the time I got halfway through the series, I knew not all the men would fit into special circumstances. Their stories reflected the challenges men face when grieving their friends. I knew this was the book to complete the series.

I'm embarrassed by my assumptions. The men in this book enjoyed deep, long-lasting friendships with men they admired and depended on. The grief they felt – and continue to feel – has directed their lives. Some made major life changes. All strive to follow the example set by their friends.

They lost their friends at different ages. Some, like those who served in the military or survived the early years of the AIDS epidemic, lost dozens or even hundreds of friends at a relatively early age. Others counted the losses as they aged. But all recognize the significance of both the friendships and their loss.

The truth is there for everyone to see: men grieve their friends every bit as deeply as women. And if you still don't believe that after reading this book, maybe you just need to listen.

Do Men Really Grieve Differently?

I consider myself a strong man and my father says be prepared to lose many in your post-50 path of life. Still, I'm a bit teary-eyed leaving this plane. R.I.P. Adam aka MCA.

– Chuck D on hearing of the death of Beastie Boy Adam Yauch

For as long as I can remember, my mother has observed, "Men are not like normal people". The context varies, but the implication is always the same: a woman's behavior is normal; a man's is not. And while you may argue her point, in the case of grief it's not an unusual observation. Men's responses to grief sometimes appear unemotional, even cold, compared to women's.

Men must be very confused about what's expected of them when they're grieving. Show your emotions? Don't show your emotions? We criticize them either way.

In the case of veterans and long-term survivors in the AIDS

community, circumstances forced them to put their grief aside. Some men in this book were stopped in their tracks by grief. Paul Sullivan had never lost anyone close to him before Terry Armour died. George Davis, well aware of Christopher Hallowell's fragile health, still felt blindsided by his death. All of the men struggled to find ways to grieve, often surprising themselves and those around them.

Some of the men you'll meet later held everything in, feeling the need to remain stoic. But they paid the price for that later, as their suppressed grief manifested itself in depression, anger and guilt.

In Dr. Elizabeth Levang's *When Men Grieve: Why Men Grieve Differently and How You Can Help*, she gives a precise explanation:

> Society has made grieving doubly hard on men. For one thing, it has given men few, if any, words to express their feelings, even though their emotions are as intense as those of their partner. Second, even if they were able to articulate their pain, most men lack a safe environment in which to share their feelings. Rather, they feel pressured to keep everything buttoned up inside or to search out opportunities to grieve in solitude. Many men would be more expressive if they did not feel that they would be violating their masculinity in the process. Like women, men want to be understood in their grief and want the freedom to grieve in their own way.

How many times have we read a book or watched on film as a young boy is told he's the man of the house after his father's death? Not only is he supposed to suppress his grief, but he has to take on the role of (at least emotionally) supporting his family.

He's not allowed to grieve in a healthy way because…he's a man.

Levang asserts that men lack a language for grief. It's not that they don't have feelings; they just don't know how to express them.

> Most women approach the work of grieving by actively expressing their emotional turmoil. Their expressiveness is visible. Men know when women grieve. Men's grief, on the other hand, is often invisible to women.

In my experience interviewing and researching men who grieve for their friends, the invisibility of men's grief is true. They may not express their grief the same way women do (assuming you can be that clear cut about gender differences). But when given the opportunity, men can be every bit as articulate as women.

So maybe we need to forget about gender roles and concentrate on a different explanation.

Personality and behavioral assessments are used in business every day: Enneagram, Meyers-Briggs, DiSC. In Dr. Kenneth Doka's book, *Disenfranchised Grief: New Directions, Challenges and Strategies for Practice*, he offers a general description of different types of grievers:

> Intuitive: Some might say an intuitive griever is typically a woman, and certainly in our society, a woman expressing her grief through crying is accepted. But this griever can also experience other physical manifestations of their grief: anxiety, confusion, inability to concentrate, physical exhaustion.
>
> Instrumental: Similarly, an instrumental griever may more likely be a man. This is someone who is reluctant to talk about their feelings, and anxious to get back to

"normal". They may also be the person who needs to do something: bring food over to the deceased's family, organize a memorial service, or clean out a closet.

Blended: A person may even possess qualities of both the intuitive and instrumental griever. In other words, they can do things and cry, too.

Dissonant: A person in conflict: a man who wants to express his grief, but feels like society won't allow that; or a woman who feels guilty for not crying a lot. These people don't feel like those around them will allow them to grieve the way that makes the most sense to them.

See yourself on the list? See people you know on the list? I'm very comfortable saying that many of the men I interviewed fell into the Dissonant category.

It's not surprising that society forces men into the Instrumental category. Men are leaders. Men take charge. Men *do things*. When forced into that category – whether it comes naturally or not – men don't have the luxury of expressing their grief in other ways.

By the time you reach a certain age, say fifty, your life seems filled with loss: grandparents, parents, aunts and uncles. The generation older than you is gone or going. Men are called upon to be pallbearers, attend to financial and legal details, pack up belongings.

But in the amazing way that humans embrace denial, we don't expect to lose those close in age: our friends. We expect those older to die before us. But middle age is when we begin to be hit hard by the loss of those friends.

There are men in this book who have lost dozens of friends at a relatively young age. Their friends died not of old age or natural causes but on a battlefield fighting a well-armed enemy or a mysterious virus. In the midst of a war no one has the luxury to call a time out to address their grief at seeing their best friend die in front of them. That's its own unique challenge, but it is also somewhat typical of dissonant grief.

Middle-aged men are not the only ones who struggle with the grief of losing a friend. A photographic exhibit, "Live for the Moment", based on a study by Dr. Genevieve Creighton at the University of British Columbia, examined how young men in Whistler, British Columbia used photography to deal with the death of a friend. The photographs taken by men aged nineteen to twenty-five, who each lost a friend to accidental death in the past year, were part of the exhibit.

What Dr. Creighton found was that even in the broad category of "accidental" deaths, there was a wide range of circumstances as well as responses.

The community of Whistler responds differently to accidental deaths "on" the mountain (skiing or snowboarding) than to those "off" the mountain. The latter, at least in these examples, tended to be drug or alcohol-related.

So, a young man could mourn his friend who died in an avalanche and be proud of him. But if he died of hypothermia, passed out in a snowdrift after leaving a bar…well, that evokes a very different type of grief.

This is the grief that's fueled by anger: how could he have been so stupid? It's not just the enormity of the loss. It's the belief that the loss was avoidable. Where the avalanche was an accident, an act of God, passing out drunk in a snowdrift was not. Blame can be assigned to the victim, and that's harder to reconcile.

Some of the young men in the study were addressing their grief for the first time. A few had already been lucky enough to reach out and accept support from those around them.

As I found in my own research, it's not that all men are instrumental grievers – focusing on "doing" something rather than talking about it. It's that doing something is the expectation – the stereotype – so most men are not encouraged to talk about their grief. As a result, this was a unique opportunity that they embraced.

Matt Gore, whose friend died in a snowdrift, used the study as a chance to give back, to help others dealing with the same type of grief. That friend's death inspired him to quit drinking and try to help others avoid the same fate as his friend.

A separate group of young men did not participate in Creighton's study because they lost friends long ago. Long-term, they handled it in different ways. Some saw that death as a wake-up call to focus and appreciate their own lives, friends and relationships. Others seemed permanently stuck, unable to "grow up" past the time when their friend died.

Creighton's study points out the need for informal grief support services for young men. One of her most fascinating suggestions is for health care providers to train coaches, instructors, bar and restaurant managers to recognize and counsel those who are grieving.

Granted, her subjects live in a ski resort town, the type of community that does not like to discuss anything as negative as a young man's death – particular if it's related to their major industry. But in a society where dealing with grief – particularly men dealing with grief – is something to be avoided, this kind of creative response is a welcome breath of fresh air. And perhaps it can serve as an example.

"It Changed My Life Forever."

I met George Davis at my first writing conference, Writer's Digest, in January of 2011. I knew no one when the conference began on Friday night, and frankly, the people I first spoke to were not particularly friendly. All that changed when I met George.

When I wrote about him on my blog I said, "If George Davis was an animal, he'd be a Labrador Retriever puppy." Openly affectionate and fun, his boundless energy and enthusiasm are contagious. By Saturday night, after we'd all pitched our manuscripts to agents and survived, a group of us who'd fallen in together during the day followed our Pied Piper, George, in search of a restaurant that would seat a party of eight without a reservation.

He led us in and out of a couple restaurants before our luck changed at Stecchino's, a lovely Italian restaurant on 9th Avenue that has since closed. The conversation – fueled by the adrenalin of the day, encouragement from the pitch slam and more than a few drinks – was loud and joyous.

But at one point, George turned to me and said, "My best friend died when I was twenty-nine and it changed my life forever."

It was so out of context that it took me a moment to respond. George was thirty-eight, so that meant this dramatic change had come ten years earlier. "Stop right there," I told him. I asked if I could interview him at another time, in a quieter place.

Several months later, back in town for Book Expo America, we met for dinner at a quieter restaurant on 9th Avenue. We sat in the back for a long time – almost three hours – as I listened to his unique and dramatic story.

The media have created the myth of the Perfect Dying Person: the saintly one who never complains despite excruciating pain; the one who protects those closest to them from the reality of their impending death. In the case of George's best friend, it was no myth.

They met as children, maybe seven or eight years old, fishing in front of Christopher's grandmother's house on Lake Champlain. In the afternoon, they pulled off their shirts and shoes before swimming down to retrieve a snagged lure. That's when George saw the scars from his new friend's open-heart surgery.

Part of being friends with Christopher Emmet Hallowell was to know that he'd always been sick. The other part of being friends with Christopher was understanding that while health challenges were an omnipresent part of his life, they didn't define him. He survived leukemia and heart and lung transplants, defying the odds again and again.

He saw himself as incredibly fortunate for having a supportive family and access to incredible health care. He never saw himself as getting a rotten deal.

He lived his too-short life to the fullest and did his best to bring his friends along for the ride. There was no time for pity, for sadness, for tears. There was only time for laughter, for excitement, for learning. He was the friend you introduced others to, and they would always become friends with him, too. He was the one whose approval you sought for your new girlfriend, as long as you were confident he wouldn't charm her away from you. Christopher was determined to live a normal life and shield his friends from the inevitable.

George remembers that attitude well:

> Fast forward about a decade (after we met) to the night at Liz Jones' Christmas party, half of Bugsy's (Christopher's) lifetime ago when I saw him for the first time after successfully having his new hardware – a new heart and a pair of lungs – installed. He was dressed to the nines as he always was for such occasions. A handsome dog, cracking jokes about survival percentages and the effects of a transplanted heart on his romantic pursuits, standing in front of the fireplace while we all huddled around and laughed and accepted what Christopher has spent so much time and energy trying to convince us all of: he was fine. No problem. No worries. Life and death? A mere bagatelle, as he wove his charm and humor around us, assuring us that it would be a waste of time to worry about him. After all, he was the life of the party!

A decade later, Christopher's lungs began to be rejected. He was also diagnosed with Hepatitis C (probably acquired as a child during a blood transfusion), which now limited his treatment options.

In the summer of 2002, his friends gathered for a pre-thirtieth birthday party (Christopher's birthday was February 3, when most of his cohorts would be scattered geographically). "It was one of the last times that Bugs presided over our collective revelry," George would later explain in his friend's eulogy. For the occasion, George and his two siblings – who'd also grown up with Christopher – read a limerick about their friend.

At three decades it's time to pause and defer

To the friend we call Bugsy, Squeak, Schmoo and Chriffer

Whether skiing or snowboarding,

Flyfishing or internetting,

You all know to whom I refer.

It was a roast, a tribute, an Irish wake of sorts. And though it may not have been acknowledged at the time, it was a way for them to express their love while Christopher was well enough to enjoy the celebration.

The last time George saw Christopher was three months before his friend's death, in the fall of 2002. He knew his friend's health was declining, but George still couldn't quite believe it. Surely he'd bounce back again. Christopher's ability to protect his friends may have made it harder to accept his death.

Obviously, Christopher was a very special person. But why had losing him changed George forever?

At the time of Christopher's death, George was living in Paris and Rome, wrapping up a teaching and coaching stint at the American School of Paris and running a startup with a partner that developed and marketed luxury vacation rentals in Europe. He wasn't wasting time and he wasn't looking for big changes. He was dating an amazing woman in New York City, and the topic of commitment occasionally provoked some soul searching.

George was in Italy working well and sleeping poorly. He knew Christopher's health was slipping from a couple of difficult telephone conversations. Then one night he dreamt that he was giving Christopher's eulogy in a tiny church in Essex, NY where George, his siblings and Christopher had all been confirmed. He woke up at 5am in a panic. A few hours later the telephone rang. His friend had died. A few days later, George flew back to eulogize his friend in that tiny church in Essex, NY where he, his siblings and Christopher had all been confirmed.

George was angry at himself for not having been there when Christopher was dying. He knew he couldn't have changed anything, but maybe he could've comforted his friend. He believed he should've known it was the end, despite the fact that Christopher had done everything he could to avoid the topic.

George reached out to others for suggestions of what to say about their friend. He included the poem he, his brother and sister had written the summer before for Christopher's birthday party.

After the funeral, George returned to Rome, but something had changed.

I've heard stories about people who made major life changes after the death of a friend. Some changed jobs or lifestyles, others moved to a new city or got married. George is the only person I know who did all of those things.

As amazing as his life was, he felt a responsibility to come home.

He walked away from a profitable business and moved back to the States. He married the woman he loved and they moved from Manhattan to the Adirondacks to renovate an historic home on the shores of Lake Champlain. She launched a green interior design firm. He began to focus on writing.

It has all the markings of a mid-life crisis, doesn't it? It's the kind of drastic change people make in their 40s or 50s or 60s, not what you might expect from a man turning 30. But theirs was a friendship that had the power to transform.

> He was the only friend I told I loved. Probably first when he was a teenager. He gave me the ability to be honest and open that way. I can count on one hand the women I know I have told I loved. It was natural to tell Christopher. Thank God he knew it. Thank God I said it.

As often happens when our lives are turned upside down, George looked for meaning. Yes, he'd turned his own life upside down, but what would his friend's legacy be?

Christopher's legacy, as it turns out, is two-fold.

First, obviously, is the change it brought to George's life.

> I'm optimistic to a fault. I always see the silver lining. I always see what can work and I think that comes at least in part from Christopher. Even when he was very sick and couldn't do the things he normally could, he found the positive, the hope, the laughter. His laughter was really powerful, though I may have been in denial the last year or so.

I can attest to that optimism. George is the first person to greet you when you walk in a room, with a big smile and a hug that lifts you off the ground. He's entertaining without demanding to be the center of attention.

The second part of Christopher's legacy was the formation of the Christopher Emmet Hallowell Foundation (http://cehfund.org). Based in their community in the Adirondacks, the fund provides financial assistance for families facing medical challenges. Money goes quickly, whether it's for hospital bills, overnight stays in hotels to be close to their loved ones, or gas for their cars. Christopher's legacy would be helping others in similar situations to his own.

"I feel his presence all the time," George said near the end of our interview. Having a cocktail on a boat, sun setting on the waters of Lake Champlain, he feels Christopher with him. And he has another drink in his memory.

More than Sports

It was an unseasonably warm February day when I walked into a quintessential Chicago sports bar, Justin's, an easy walk from Wrigley Field. The music was semi-loud, the decor mostly made up of autographed memorabilia from various players. Roseanne Tellez of CBS2 Chicago had told Paul Sullivan, who covers the Cubs for the *Chicago Tribune*, about my interview with her for my book (*Friend Grief in the Workplace: More Than an Empty Cubicle*) and now Paul wanted to meet with me.

Roseanne's on-air partner and friend, Randy Salerno, died in a snowmobiling accident. But earlier, when Paul's friend Terry Armour died of a heart attack, Randy emailed Paul about Terry:

> The guy always made me laugh. I guess that's the best thing you can say about somebody.

It was Paul's suggestion that we meet at Justin's, where he and his friend spent a lot of time. The manager stopped by our table when Paul first arrived and was pleased that we were going to talk about Terry. Unwittingly, I'd sat down very close to a shrine to Terry, a large plaque covered with photos of him that hung on the wall just past the end of the bar. He was really part of the conversation now.

There could not have been an odder couple than Terry and Paul. Terry was an outgoing, physically imposing, 6'4", African-American man. To say that he was larger than life would be an understatement. Paul is a much shorter, quieter, white guy. They met in December, 1981, while they were both copy clerks in the *Tribune* newsroom. They quickly became drinking buddies and friends until Terry's death twenty-six years later, almost to the day.

Their lives as single men on the North Side of Chicago revolved around work. Paul covered the Cubs and Terry covered the Bulls during their championship streak in the 1990's before moving on to the celebrity beat in 1999.

Terry's dream was to cover the White Sox while Paul covered the Cubs. Then, he told him, they could write dueling columns. Terry could write "Cubs suck" and Sullivan could write "Sox suck".

They did everything together. Terry would join Paul during Cubs spring training in Arizona. They smoked cigars in Paul's hotel room in Houston after the Sox won the World Series in 2005. They were together when Terry was arrested at the Cell (US Cellular Field, home of the White Sox) for punching an obnoxious Cubs fan.

Justin's being a "Cheers" kind of place, the two men made it a second home. They sat at the same bar stools three or four times a week for several years.

Terry was the kind of person that strangers and friends alike gravitated towards. He knew everyone and treated the security guard in the Tribune Tower with the same respect as Michael Jordan. His death was mourned by thousands who had never met him.

A year or so before he died, two of Terry's close friends died a day apart, and he was deeply affected. One death was somewhat expected, the other was not. Those deaths were the first in their age group of men in their forties, something that often shocks people into considering their mortality for the first time. Terry decided to enjoy life even more.

One day right after Christmas 2007, Paul returned home from lunch to find a message on his answering machine to call his boss right away. He assumed it was an assignment, and was not eager to return the call as he'd had a few drinks. But he did call, and his boss told him Terry Armour had collapsed in the *Tribune* offices and died in the ambulance en route to the hospital. He was forty-six. Paul's first reaction was "Nah...not real."

Until that day, no one close to Paul Sullivan had died: not family (his mother would die less than a year later), not close friends. He had no experience with grief, and it left him adrift. Like many men, he felt compelled to do something. But not being a family member, he ran up against what many people in his situation also experience: they're not in control.

He went over to Terry's apartment, heartbroken to see Terry's wife so shattered. He wanted to do something, organize something, fix something. He needed something to hold onto and there was nothing, not even a memorial service until months later.

A few days after Terry's death, Paul took it upon himself to box up the things in his friend's desk at work. It was the first constructive thing he'd been able to do. People came by to talk about Terry, share stories. The year before, Terry had also cleaned out a dead friend's desk, so to Paul it felt appropriate. Plus, he felt protective of Terry's stuff.

Eventually, Terry's wife gave Paul some of his friend's baseball caps. He wore them in tribute when he made reports on TV. It was important to have something of Terry's, a physical reminder of his existence and their friendship.

Back in 1993, Paul had one of those answering machines with the little tapes. At some point it broke and he threw the tape in a box. One day after Terry died, he played the tape. It was full of dozens of messages from his friend: weird, funny, profane. Hearing his friend's voice, the voice he'd never hear again in person, did not make him sad. It made him happy.

The two men had parallel careers for a while, until Terry's took off. But their friendship remained the same. Paul admitted to possibly being a little jealous about his friend's success, but it seemed impossible to hold a grudge against his best friend.

Paul feels his friend's presence in the places they shared. Sometimes it's sitting at the bar at Justin's. Sometimes when something stupid happens at deadline, Paul believes his friend is messing with him. And even though Terry isn't actually there, Paul wishes he was.

After Terry died, a mutual friend who'd joined both men at Cubs spring training now arrived in Arizona alone. Terry was not far from their thoughts, never more so than when the second bedroom in the condo where Paul was staying became infested with bees that burrowed into the wall. Even while calling the exterminator they kept saying, "Damn you, Terry." Their friend would've seen a lot of humor in it, and luckily they did too.

Paul finally found a way to do something lasting. He and other friends of Terry get together in January at a place that Terry liked, such as Buddy Guy's jazz club to talk about their friend and how things have changed.

Justin's is closed now, so Paul has to find another place to watch baseball. But I have no doubt his friend will be there, too, at the bar stool next to him, still insisting "Cubs suck".

How Deep Are Their Friendships?

Jim Eigo and I shared a booth in a diner a few blocks south of Lincoln Center. I met Jim at my first ACT UP/NY meeting in April, 2013. He's physically imposing: tall with a lean, athletic body. He reminds me a little of Mr. Clean, with a sometimes stern expression that I would never want directed towards me.

Jim is a writer, editor and noted activist. Like many who have been in the AIDS community from the early days, he possesses a breadth of knowledge that is stunning. He's responsible for projects as varied as reforms of AIDS drug regulations and grant applications to fund ACT UP outreach efforts.

I've heard Jim speak of friends who died of AIDS, including in the Academy Award-nominated documentary *How To Survive A Plague*. But I told him I didn't want to talk about those friends. I wanted to hear about his friends who died of something other than AIDS. There were too many who died of AIDS anyway. It would've taken days to acknowledge them all.

The first friend he talked about was not a gay man. It was an older woman who became his mentor when he was studying playwriting at Cal Arts in the 1970s.

Ruby Cohn was two years older than Jim's mother, a woman who, in her lifetime, played basketball, learned radar and went to Paris after World War II.

By the time they met, Ruby was the doyenne of West Coast theater critics, and a renowned critic and friend of Samuel Beckett. One of Ruby's talents was, as Jim put it, "enabling relationships". At the weekly salon she held at Cal Arts, one could always find an interesting assortment of people, such as Sally Jacobs, Peter Brooks' designer on such legendary productions as *Marat/Sade* and *A Midsummer Night's Dream.*

In Ruby, Jim found a mentor, a friend and a Jewish mother. She paid his rent for four years because "I believe in you".

The last time he saw her was 2005, ten years after she'd been diagnosed with Parkinson's. Her health declined slowly. Jim kept her up to date on the New York theatre scene by email because talking on the phone became difficult for her.

The longer Jim spoke of her the more emotional he became. Ruby was one of those friends whose support and encouragement gives us the confidence to fully be ourselves. And when they're gone, the loss is not just of the friendship, but a piece of ourselves. Her belief in his talent, in his goodness, in his potential made him the man he is today. And while he misses her deeply, his grief is very different than for his friend Robert.

Robert was, like Jim, a member of ACT UP/New York at a time when the media warned against "the gay plague". He and Jim had much in common besides their shared passion for ending the epidemic. Robert was a writer in the arts, including *Time Out NY*, and a filmmaker. They enjoyed long, passionate discussions about the arts.

Jim left ACT UP in 1992. The group was experiencing growing pains common to even the most successful grassroots movements. Jim's interests within the AIDS community had evolved to focus on healthcare as a right, something that was too broad-based for the direction of the committee that became the Treatment Action Group (TAG). Like many, he was exhausted, and despite being a passionate, compelling public speaker, Jim's actually rather shy. He needed a break, but not a complete break. Robert was the person from ACT UP he saw the most.

The way Jim talked about Robert – as opposed to Ruby – was very different. Jim and Ruby shared a passion for the arts. She was an older woman, a mentor, a guide. His voice hinted at an ingrained respect for older people, acknowledging that her death was the end of an important period in his life.

Jim and Robert were peers marching together – two gay men who were HIV-negative – fighting for the lives of their friends. Robert's death also brought tears to Jim's eyes, because it wasn't AIDS that killed him.

On a trip to Georgia, Robert was in a car accident that resulted in a concussion. The complications from his concussion made managing his OCD impossible. He was in so much pain, Robert's boyfriend told Jim, not just physically.

Over the next few months, Jim saw his friend only a few times, although they lived close to each other. The last time Robert brushed him off and Jim didn't understand why.

One day Robert jumped off the roof of his building.

Jim's voice cracked as he spoke. "We were so close but I didn't know what he was going through." His inability to understand, to help his friend, haunted him.

There we were, still sitting in the booth in that diner near Columbus Circle. I stopped typing and looked across the table at Jim. "You couldn't know," I told him. "He didn't know how to explain what he was going through." I told him about my own experience with post-concussive syndrome and how frustrating it had been to describe what I was feeling. "You couldn't help him because Robert didn't know what he needed or how to ask for help. It wasn't your fault."

Jim stared at me. "No one's ever understood this."

"What ifs" are not uncommon after a suicide. They're not uncommon among people in the AIDS community who carry the virus and those who don't. Survivor guilt, especially for men, is rooted in the shame of feeling powerless: "I should've *known*."

It's not surprising, then, that men seek ways to be helpful when a friend is dying. They may understand intellectually that they can't save their friend, but emotionally...even small, seemingly insignificant gestures can mean a lot later on. Such was the friendship Mike and Arthur had with Bob.

Mike Genovese and Arthur Rosenberg have been friends since 1969. I met them the following year when I was in the theatre conservatory at Webster College (now Webster University). My teachers were actors in the Repertory Theatre of St. Louis, in residence at Webster. Mike Genovese was my acting teacher and I had Arthur Rosenberg for voice and speech.

Both men eventually wound up in Los Angeles. Mike is still acting and involved in SAG-AFTRA. But Arthur's life took a major turn some years ago when he became a rabbi, the Leonard Nimoy Palliative Care Chaplain at the Motion Picture and Television Fund (MPTF) in Woodland Hills. He won't be offended if I say I never expected to see him in this new role, but it suits him.

There was an odd bit of serendipity to our visit at his office. Initially we talked about the differences he sees in grief for a parent, say, and grief for a friend. We spoke of how the roles we assume in our families can sometimes inhibit healthy grieving. One advantage to friendship is that we are largely unconstrained by rigid expectations. But suddenly he mentioned the name of a friend, Bob Darnell, another actor who'd been in the repertory company at Webster. Mike – who I was staying with – had mentioned him to me, too.

Arthur brought up Bob without explanation. "You know," I told him. "Mike opened his calendar and showed me Bob's name. He writes down the names of some of his friends on the anniversary of the day they died."

"It was yesterday," Arthur realized. "Yesterday was the anniversary."

The three men met at Webster, all young actors performing with the professional company and teaching in the conservatory. Arthur described Bob, who looked a lot like Jim Croce, as "a human tornado" but a grounded person, too. "He taught me about what to take seriously."

When Bob was diagnosed with stage 4 brain cancer, Mike and Arthur were there for him. There was no cure, only multiple surgeries. With each surgery, he'd lose more of the right side of his brain. They did what they could do, sometimes just taking him out for the pancakes he craved.

When the end was near and Bob's wife was working out of town, his friends took over his hospital room. They staged a variety show – jokes, singing, monologues – to keep him alert and entertained until she could join him. His death was a profound loss for both men.

They organized a hell of a party in Bob's memory, with lots of single malt whiskey. It was their way of managing his death and their grief, though Arthur insisted they would've done it differently at an older age. It would've been quieter, though probably still with lots of single malt whiskey. But they would've felt less of a need to "do something".

I asked Arthur, as I've asked everyone I've interviewed for my books, if he felt Bob's presence. Though he insisted he didn't, not like in the sense of a hologram appearing before him, he admitted to thinking of him often. "I ask myself 'What would Bob say?'"

But even more surprising than the serendipitous discussion about Bob Darnell, was one of the last things Arthur said was about his friendship with Mike.

He and Mike are very different. Mike grew up in St. Louis, Catholic and Italian. Arthur grew up in New York, Jewish. But their friendship of more than four decades is a perfect match of personalities. He insisted in all that time they've never had a cross word for each other, and as unlikely as that sounds, I believe him. Just like I believed him when he said, "I'll deal with my own death better than Mike's."

"All My Friends Are Dead."

That was the first thing Pierre Jalbert said to me when we settled in at his dining room table. We were at the home he built in the Beverly Glen section of Los Angeles for our first conversation about his amazing life: a life made possible by friends long gone.

At eighty-seven and still recuperating from a stroke, Pierre definitely moved more slowly than he had when we first met almost thirty years earlier. I was greeted with a gentle hug and kiss on both cheeks. His eyes still twinkled when he flirted or teased. He complained only that his grey and white hair wasn't long enough for a ponytail. Now and then he'd become frustrated that he couldn't remember the name of someone he knew sixty years earlier. But he was still handsome enough to make me blush whenever he touched my arm to make a point.

It was one of those perfect California days: bright sun, reasonable temperature, light wind. It was quiet, our location in the back of the house protecting us from the noise of cars speeding up and down the Glen.

"We're not all dead," I reminded him and he shrugged, not quite willing to agree.

As Pierre recounted the details of a life that would make a fabulous, if sometimes unbelievable film, he paused now and then to credit a friend.

He grew up in Quebec, an accomplished competitive skier by the age of 14. In 1945, at the age of 20, he was struck with rheumatic fever. His doctor told Pierre he'd never ski again. He laughed at him and simply refused to believe it. After the war, he enrolled at Laval University and returned to skiing. He rose through the ranks to become Canadian national junior champion in all four downhill ski events in 1947. In 1948 he was named captain of the Canadian ski team, headed to St. Moritz, Switzerland, for the first Winter Olympics after the war.

Pierre was not, at eighty-seven, a man with many regrets. In fact, I never heard him complain about any setback. Whether it was belief in Buddhism or just his personality, he saw no permanent downside to anything, even what happened to him on the mountain two days before the opening ceremonies.

He shattered his leg in a training run, an injury that would leave that leg an inch shorter than the other, and cause chronic pain for the rest of his life. Not only was his dream of winning a medal dashed, but also the dream of competing at all. Again, the doctors told him he'd never ski again.

"Weren't you depressed?" I interrupted him, as he moved quickly to the next part of the story.

"Sure," he agreed. "For about a week."

It was while he lay in the hospital in St. Moritz that a new friend visited him, actress Norma Shearer and her husband (years later Pierre and his wife would be married in Shearer's living room). They invited him and the only Australian skier, also recuperating from a similar injury, to join them in Paris when they were able to travel. And really, how could he say no?

While he was happy there for two years working in business, an unexpected offer tempted him to leave. Norma Shearer was back in Paris, with her daughter from her marriage to Irving Thalberg, and invited Pierre to join them for dinner. There, Norma asked him to move to Sun Valley, Idaho to become a private ski instructor. He admitted that he stayed up all night, just wandering around the quiet city, weighing the pros and cons, before agreeing to this new adventure.

Pierre found that he loved teaching and was in great demand. He didn't just teach the mechanics of skiing down a mountain. He focused on helping his students lose their fears and enjoy the thrill. He was living on a mountain, doing what he loved, when he encountered another setback. It turns out he's one of those creative people who are not good with details, so one day he found himself being deported back to Quebec for failure to obtain the proper work visa.

The other ski instructors gave him a "deportation party" the night before he had to leave. One of the guests was a student of his, Gordon McLain, who was a member of the Harris Bank family. Gordon promised to sponsor Pierre's legal return and he kept his word. On May 15, 1951, thanks to Gordon being his "godfather", Pierre was back in the United States for good, this time back in Los Angeles

Pierre now returned to doing what he'd loved back home: sound editing and syncing dialogue post-production. He worked on films such as *Mutiny on the Bounty* and *The Godfather*. In fact, Pierre was brought in to give feedback on the latter. When you watch the iconic scene of the rival mobsters being executed while Michael Corleone performs his godfather duties in church, you can thank Pierre for the idea.

While working at MGM in 1961 he got a call from an agent to audition for a new television show, *Combat!* He wasn't looking for acting work, but agreed. For the next five years – thanks to MGM granting him a leave of absence – he played Caje on the series. That was how I knew about him: I was a fan. But an odd turn of events brought my two best friends and me to his home, along with one of the other actors on the show, in the mid-80s.

It was two years after their former co-star Vic Morrow was killed in a horrific accident on the set of *Twilight Zone: The Movie*. Pierre's wife later said that that night was the first time he and Jack talked about Vic. They talked at length that night about their memories of working together and helping each other.

When *Combat!* began, a bargain was struck: Pierre would teach Vic about editing and Vic would help Pierre with his acting. A working relationship and friendship were formed, one that Pierre credited for improving his acting skills.

"I wouldn't be where I am without my friends," Pierre said more than once during our conversation. Though he was certainly helped in his career by his refusal to burn bridges, he didn't give that a lot of weight. Nor did he credit his work ethic or talent. He didn't take those things for granted; he just didn't think they were the reason for his success. His friends, the ones who appeared at odd moments – in a mountain resort hospital or a deportation going away party – were the ones who directed his life.

He spoke, then, fondly of all of them, only giving in to a tear or two when Vic's name came up. The anger was still there, the grief of the loss of a man who was so important to him still fresh in some ways almost three decades later.

He was lucky, he insisted, to be guided by them.

If there was any regret, it was for losing track of Gordon. They saw each other only sporadically over the years, and because he had come from a prominent Chicago family, I offered to do a little research on him when I returned home. What I found was of interest to Pierre, but it was too late to resolve anything.

I never brought up friends during our conversations. My intent was really to just get him to tell his life story. I never asked him about his friendships. I let him guide the flow of discussion.

It always revolved around friends – Norma, Gordon, Vic – the men and women who popped into his life at critical moments and led him in new, exciting directions. Men and women who were long gone, but whose name or photo sparked a twinkle in his eyes and joy in his voice. And always, always, it came back to his gratitude to those friends for guiding him, supporting him and giving him a life that would make a fabulous movie.

"Ask God to Love Him, Too."

There were a lot of really bad TV movies in the 1970s, though I confess to a weakness for almost all of them. The scripts were awful, the acting was awful, and the clothes were worse than that. But one stands out, a film based on the true story of two professional football players, Brian Piccolo and Gale Sayers of the Chicago Bears. If you're old enough to remember *Brian's Song*, the first few bars of the theme music will immediately bring to mind the slow-motion sight of Billy Dee Williams and James Caan running laps. If there is a human being on the face of the earth who can watch this movie without crying, I haven't met them.

As Jeannie Morris recounts in *Brian Piccolo: A Short Season*, their unlikely friendship was full of stereotypical male bonding: good-natured insults, dares, roughhousing.

Only 5'11" and 190 pounds, Brian led the nation in rushing and scoring as a senior at Wake Forest University in 1964. And though he beat Gale, the two-time All-American in those categories, he wasn't drafted. The Bears signed him as a free agent.

He always believed in being in the right place at the right time, though signing onto a team that already drafted Gale didn't fit that definition. Brian spent most of his four seasons with the Bears in Gale's shadow.

But even before they became friends, Brian didn't resent the spotlight on Gale. Those who played with him say he never had a bad word to say about anyone. He found humor in situations that were deadly serious. He was passionate about football, but he never forgot that friends and family were more important.

And then in 1967 came a first for the Bears: a black player and a white player rooming together. Gale was approached by management with the idea, and he asked for Brian, though they weren't close friends. Their personalities could have not have been more different. Gale was quiet, serious, focused. Brian was the definition of "scrappy". But their friendship on and off the field deepened.

In 1969, a persistent cough and shortness of breath revealed a startling diagnosis: Brian had cancer. Embryonal cell carcinoma is an aggressive form of germ cell testicular cancer, and it had spread to his chest cavity. Surgery removed his left lung and pectoral muscle, and though initial treatments were promising, the cancer spread to his liver and other organs.

Gale, by virtue of his comeback from knee surgery, was awarded the George S. Halas Award for being the most courageous football player in the 1969 season. It's a prestigious award, named for the founder of the Chicago Bears, one that rewards perseverance in the face of severe challenges, rather than statistics racked up on the field. But Gale disagreed with who had been named the recipient. And in his brief acceptance speech, he explained why:

> He has the heart of a giant and that rare form of courage that allows him to kid himself and his opponent – cancer. He has the mental attitude that makes me proud to have a friend who spells out the word "courage" twenty-four hours a day every day of his life. You flatter me by giving me this award, but I tell you that I accept it for Brian Piccolo. It is mine tonight, it is Brian Piccolo's tomorrow…I love Brian Piccolo, and I'd like to ask all of you to love him, too. Tonight when you hit your knees, please ask God to love him.

Brian didn't know Gale was going to make that speech about him. When he found out, though gravely ill, he found humor in it, telling Gale if he'd been there he would've given him a kiss. That was Brian: making jokes, putting others at ease.

Brian Piccolo died about a month later, on June 16, 1970. He was twenty-six.

The tributes to him were many. But two stand out among the schools and scholarships named for him.

The Chicago Bears give the Brian Piccolo Award every season to a rookie and a veteran who best exemplify the courage, loyalty, teamwork, dedication and sense of humor of the running back who died too soon. For some time now, the players are men who were born after he died. But in their acceptance speeches it's clear they understand the legacy of #41.

Perhaps the greatest tribute to him comes from the remarkable success of the Brian Piccolo Fund. It's often the case when someone dies of an incurable disease that friends are motivated to donate money for research. Sometimes they support organizations that are already established. In this case, because his particular type of cancer was so rare, they started their own.

The Brian Piccolo Cancer Research Fund initially was formed to find a cure for embryonal cell carcinoma. In 1969, a diagnosis was a death sentence. Thanks to the millions of dollars raised, that once deadly form of cancer has a 95% survival rate. The fund now focuses its attention on breast cancer research.

Few people remember Brian Piccolo's football statistics. Some remember Gale's. But most people, when hearing one name or the other, still connect the two unlikely roommates.

Veterans of Two Very Different Wars

When I was working on *Friend Grief and the Military: Band of Friends*, a thought kept popping into my head: "This sounds familiar". There were times when I thought I had already written a passage, when clearly I had not. It took a while, but I finally figured it out.

The one thing that complicates grief the most for people on the battle field is that they cannot take time to grieve when their friends are killed. They have to step over the bodies and keep fighting. They have to suppress their grief in the short-term in order to survive themselves. That's just the way it is.

Gay men in the AIDS community delayed their grief because they had to: they had to take care of themselves and their friends, they had to fight for basic rights of housing and health care, they had to fight a war – no time to enjoy the luxury of grieving dozens, or even hundreds, of friends.

There are striking similarities between those who have been affected by AIDS and those who have served our country in the military. Both groups suffer from survivor guilt, risk of suicide, complicated health issues and stigma. Both groups have kept their experiences to themselves, only willing to talk about the war many years later. Both share strong support communities even while battling crippling loneliness.

Imagine if the war in Vietnam or Iraq or Afghanistan had dragged on for thirty years, with no end in sight. That's what it's like to be a veteran of the war against AIDS. Sometimes it feels like you're winning, sometimes you feel like you're losing. Sometimes you're on the front lines, sometimes you're sent back for a brief furlough before redeploying. Maybe you mustered out. But the war goes on.

Jim Eigo lives in the East Village. One of the most moving things he said to me was about his walk over to the Monday night ACT UP meetings at the LGBT Center in the West Village. "I see ghosts," he explained. He walks across Manhattan and sees the ghosts of his past: a building where a friend lived, bars where they partied into the night, a corner where long-dead fellow AIDS activists staged an action. For many like Jim who stayed in New York, it's like living in a battlefield, the ghosts of fallen comrades all around you.

When I've mentioned to people that I see a lot of similarities between veterans of war and long-term survivors in the AIDS community I'm usually met with blank stares. It's understandable. What could these two groups have in common, other than watching their friends die? As it turns out, they share a lot.

Benjamin Heim Shepard's book *Rebel Friendships: "Outsider" Networks and Social Movements* looks at "affinity groups": sometimes unlikely collections of individuals united in a common cause. It seems a good definition for both veterans and gay men in the AIDS community.

In my book on the military, I explained the issue of "moral injury". More than post-traumatic stress (PTSD) – which is also prevalent in both groups – moral injury represents internal conflicts that can contribute to unresolved grief. Some examples of moral injury in both groups include:

> Doing something that causes harm or death to a friend.
>
> Failing to provide adequate medical care to a friend, resulting in permanent injury or death.
>
> Doing something (under explicit orders or by assumption) that you believe is morally wrong.
>
> Questioning the justification for your actions, including your belief system.
>
> Surviving when your friend died.

(Although women are also at risk for moral injury, for our purposes here, we'll discuss men only.)

The consequences of these perceived "failings" are many.

It's no secret that suicide is on the rise in the veteran community. But few people realize that it is also a serious issue for long-term survivors in the AIDS community. What leads men in both groups to survive unimaginable horrors, only to take their own lives once that danger has passed?

Two men who are all too familiar with these dangers are Brian Kinsella and Jeff Berry. Brian helped found Stop Soldier Suicide, an organization dedicated to supporting veterans at risk with a 24/7 hotline. Jeff Berry was part of a group that started The Reunion Project to address the needs of long-term survivors in the AIDS community. Both men will both give you the same answer to why their peers are at risk for suicide: isolation.

When the immediate danger has passed – when you're home from the war or the AIDS epidemic has slowed down – you need to heal. For too many men, talking about their experiences is not a consideration. People who weren't there want to hear about the killing and the excitement, but that's not what most veterans want to relive upon their return home. They retreat into themselves, which in the short-term is not a bad thing. Healing takes many forms. The problems arise when the isolation becomes a way of life.

The widely advertised statistic that twenty-two veterans and one active-duty member of the military are lost to suicide every day is based on data from only twenty-three states, and the methodology of that data does not necessarily include everyone. It depends on accurate reporting by law enforcement and surviving families. A more accurate accounting would prove about fifty suicides a day – more than 18,000 a year. No one knows what the number is in the AIDS community.

After the anti-retroviral cocktail of drugs became available in 1996, AIDS no longer meant an instant death sentence. People who were actively dying were given the new drugs, resulting in what has been called "The Lazarus Effect". The deaths slowed down to a trickle. The war, in a sense, was over.

There's a reason why VFW halls, Dryhootch and other veterans' groups exist: for vets to share experiences no one else can imagine. They meet formally and informally with the only people they believe understand how they feel. They have a "home" to go to when they need support. The groups are most beneficial when they are specific to certain conflicts. Returning Vietnam vets did not feel welcomed in groups filled with veterans of WWII and Korea, because their experiences were so radically different. So they – as well as vets from more recent conflicts – founded groups that could specifically relate to their own needs.

Until recently, there were no such groups in the AIDS community. After 1996, the gains in medical treatment were offset by a dramatic loss of community. Gay men who were HIV-positive were now able to be more independent. Whether you were HIV positive or negative, in the first fifteen years of the epidemic there was a palpable sense of shared purpose. Gay men were united in ways no one could've predicted, because their lives – and those of their friends – were on the line.

Those of us who remember the dark early days have been criticized as being nostalgic. And though it's offensive to think that anyone would want to return to the devastation of that time, there is a grain of truth in the criticism. The AIDS community in many ways fell apart after 1996, when the anti-retroviral drugs changed everything, as one of the long-term survivors in Perry Halkaitis' *The AIDS Generation: Stories of Survival and Resilience* laments:

> The loss and devastation was matched in later years by the disbanding of the gay community. We got a pill. Stay away from them and you'll be fine. We totally left lesbians in the dust, just turned on them after they held our hands while we died. I do yearn for the community of the past in the very worst way and hope in my lifetime to see it again under much happier circumstances. I feel that I don't fit in anywhere in the gay community now. Then we were all one, accepting of each other, and that is no longer the case.

Attendance at ACT UP meetings plummeted. AIDS service organizations merged or closed their doors. Weekly fundraisers at gay bars were no longer necessary. Thanks, too, to advances in diagnosis and prevention, there were fewer gay men being diagnosed with AIDS. And those who had it were now living healthy, productive lives. The intense, urgent, immediate crisis was over.

So why is that bad?

Both groups of men were previously identified by their "uniforms". For the military, it was a literal uniform. For gay men with AIDS it was the obvious lesions of Kaposi's sarcoma on a skeletal body. But now, after their respective wars, they no longer stand out. They look like other men. They function more or less like other men. But inside, they're not. One only needs to realize that more veterans of the Falklands War have died of suicide than during the conflict itself to understand that something very disturbing is happening.

They carry with them the grief and guilt for their friends who died: the friends they could not save. They give themselves little credit for surviving because they're haunted by what they could not do for those who died.

Now and then the news outlets report the awarding of a Medal of Honor, a distinction given to only the bravest of the brave. Often the ceremony at the White House is televised live, so that all can witness the recognition these veterans so richly deserve.

The circumstances of their bravery vary. Most were seriously wounded when they found the strength to save their comrades. But one aspect of their acceptance speeches does not vary: honoring those they could not save. It matters less that they killed the enemy, secured strategic positions or saved most of the men and women in their unit. They always mention the ones who died in battle – sometimes by name. "Leave no one behind" is their motto. In their minds, they failed to fulfill their duty. Only other veterans understand why they do not celebrate their accomplishment.

In late 2014 I attended a meeting at Gay Men's Health Crisis

(GMHC) in New York. It was structured as a listening session, so that GMHC could identify the needs of long-term survivors. Time and again, one word stood out: isolation.

Just like many veterans, long-term survivors struggle to understand why they survived and their friends did not. Like many veterans, their questions not only go unanswered, but are dismissed by those outside their community: "Who cares? You're alive. That's all that matters."

We expect to watch our friends die as we age. But both groups of men lost dozens – even hundreds – of friends when they were in their twenties or thirties. They knew they could also die young. Many expected to die young. So it's not that surprising that as they reach their forties, fifties and beyond, that unresolved grief resurfaces.

But without a close-knit community to support them, they isolate themselves. They refuse to discuss their needs with anyone who wasn't there, too. They refuse to discuss their needs, period. They become trapped in an endless loop of regrets, guilt and grief. For many, suicide seems to become a reasonable option.

Jeff Berry found that grief is a topic that some long-term survivors are just now starting to address. The twenty years since the anti-retroviral drugs were introduced has given them enough time removed to find some perspective and distance. Others are still resistant. But even men in the gay community who are HIV-negative express survivor guilt. They survived, yes, but because they're not living with the virus, they're even less likely to believe they need support.

He expressed a common theme of survivor guilt in the community: they didn't know how to help. It's all clear now: how to avoid infection, how to treat it, how to live a healthy life with HIV. But in the 80's in particular, we were flying blind. It's not very logical to blame ourselves for not knowing what no one else knew, either. But logic doesn't often enter into the world of grief. As Jeff Goins observed in his own experience of grieving two friends,

> When someone we know dies, we want to try to understand why, and that desire can create a lot of confusion. But there is a comfort in knowing that when you lose someone, in spite of what you feel, you're not alone.

That's a powerful realization: that others share your experience of grieving a friend.

Forming groups like Iraq and Afghanistan Veterans of America and Stop Soldier Suicide have given recently returning military the resources they need. In them veterans find likeminded people who share experiences that civilians can only imagine. They can begin to address their grief in healthy ways. I would submit that this new generation of veterans under the age of forty has driven the movement to ensure that their comrades receive the support only possible from someone who's been there too. They're not content to wait for the backlog at the VA to lessen. They're used to taking action so they've channeled their training and experiences into helping others address their grief and lead healthy lives without suffering unnecessarily from bureaucratic delays.

There's an intensity to war, no matter the enemy. The adrenalin, the risk, the constant danger: every sense is heightened. The return to civilian – "normal" – life can be confusing and disappointing, even without addressing grief.

That's not the case with both groups…is it? What inspired the long-term survivor movement in the AIDS community? Perry Halkitis's 2014 study of a group of gay men in New York has certainly brought attention to the needs of this previously invisible group. But I believe the death of former ACT UP member Spencer Cox served as a dramatic wake-up call.

Spencer was loved and respected by many for his activism. When he died in 2012 it was a shock. He was on the cocktail. He was fine. Wasn't he?

Actually, no.

Despite his renewed enthusiasm for life that was sparked by his participation in the Academy Award-nominated documentary *How to Survive a Plague*, he was literally and figuratively isolated. He moved back to New York early in 2012, but priced out of his old neighborhood, he found an apartment in Inwood, about 150 blocks north at the opposite end of Manhattan. His health and finances deteriorated, and in December of that year, he died. His situation – physically isolated with the challenges of aging with HIV – was not that unusual. But it's one that until then had been largely unknown, or at least unacknowledged.

That is not to imply that he took his own life. There is little evidence to support that theory. But the challenges he faced are not easily faced alone, so there are no easy answers.

His funeral brought together friends and colleagues who had lost touch with each other, that urgent need for activism having faded long ago. Their grief – just like the grief that drove veterans to create organizations like Stop Soldier Suicide – sparked a renewed commitment to serve their community.

Now the room where ACT UP meets every Monday night is full. People who had been silent for years are now appearing on TV, writing editorials and organizing actions. Some of it is driven by those veterans, gay men now in their fifties and sixties who are determined to put an end to the epidemic once and for all. And their renewed spirit is inspiring a new generation of activists who also believe that an AIDS-free generation is within our grasp.

Like military veterans, the older ones are still doing it for their friends: the dozens – hundreds – that died before anyone could help them. And they're doing it so this younger generation is not faced with the same kind of devastation and loss. They're channeling their grief into action: that stereotypically male way of behaving. And this time they're determined to end the war, once and for all.

A Life Dedicated to Their Friends

As we saw at the beginning of the book, men are perceived to be "doers" when it comes to grief. They and those around them expect grief to be fixed in some way. They expect action. They expect results.

So it's not surprising that many men, in response to losing their friend, change in dramatic ways. The timing can be crucial. They've reached a certain age, a certain station in life. Maybe they were already restless, searching for some kind of renewed purpose. But all will say that they changed course because of their friend: the way that person lived and the hole they left behind. And while George Davis may have been an extreme example, he's not alone when it comes to making major life changes.

Concussions are a serious issue. Believe me, I know: I had one in 2009 and I still deal with the fallout every day. I had no fracture, no swelling, no bleeding. I did not lose consciousness. I'm able to function pretty well most of the time, and I'm not getting worse. But many athletes are not so lucky. One such athlete was Steve

Montador, who suffered multiple concussions during his ten-year NHL career. He was found dead of natural causes in 2015.

How does one die of natural causes at thirty-five? An autopsy of his brain found severe chronic traumatic encephalopathy. Not diagnosed as often in hockey players, it's devastated many professional football players.

"You could see something was going on with his brain other than him falling out of sobriety," said his friend and former Chicago Blackhawks teammate, Daniel Carcillo.

So when Daniel suffered his second (documented) concussion just weeks later, you have to assume the death of his friend weighed even heavier. In late April he was cleared to return to the ice, where his team won their third Stanley Cup championship in six years.

It's a tradition that the team members get to spend a day with Lord Stanley's cup. They can take it home, visit a children's hospital, go to a baseball game. You can pose your baby in the cup or drink beer out of it.

Daniel's cup celebration came at the beginning of September. He gave a party, but one with a very special purpose. Daniel, you see, had retired from hockey. Before the party he'd announced:

> Today, I'm retiring from the National Hockey League. My immediate goal is to help athletes transition to the next phase of their life – whether it's continuing education, finding internships with companies, or networking with other athletes who are dealing with the same issues. My mission is to help guys who are dealing with anxiety, depression, and uncertainty about their future. Not down the line, not next week, but right now.

He'd seen first-hand the challenges Steve faced: not just the multiple concussions, but the complications of moving from a fast-paced, public life to one of near-obscurity. With luck, athletes can live forty or fifty years after retirement. But for many, what time they have after retirement is clouded by post-concussive issues and substance abuse, problems too overwhelming to address alone.

As happens more often than you might imagine, the death of a friend inspired Daniel to start Chapter 5 – Steve wore number 5 – an organization to help professional athletes transition from the limelight to real life.

So Daniel's Stanley Cup party was a fundraiser for three hundred Blackhawks fans who could bid on hockey-related items, including a Blackhawks jersey signed by the entire championship team. They had the chance to have their picture taken with Lord Stanley's cup (for those who aren't hockey fanatics, there is nothing comparable in other sports).

It would've been easy to simply retire quietly and return to a less-demanding life. Daniel could spend more time with his infant son, only three months older than Steve's baby boy, born just four days after he died.

But instead, his friend's death gave him a new life. One with a purpose and a passion that was certainly not anything he could've predicted. But it's evident this is a man at peace: with his decision to retire and with the way he now lives his life, in honor of his friend.

All of the men in this book were changed forever by the death of their friend(s). All of them will tell you that their friends were more important to them than the other way around. All of them believe that the life they still lead is in some ways – deliberately or not – dedicated to making that friend proud of them.

For those in the military and AIDS community, the need to share those memories is even more intense. But all of the men whose stories you've just read define their mission in life as ensuring that those friends – the ones they outlived, even if they don't know why – are remembered and honored.

Mark Liebenow wrote in *Huffington Post* about why it was important for Vice President Joe Biden to publicly share his grief for his son, Beau. He gave five reasons, but as far as I was concerned, he could've stopped at #1:

"He's a man."

Final Thoughts

> Even though I've lost a lot of dear, dear friends…It was a learning experience. And each one, I learned something different about me, that I can be residual. I can be forceful. I can be determined, and I'm a good fighter. And I'm going to be in it for the long haul.
>
> — Antoine, in *The AIDS Generation: Stories of Survival and Resilience*

This book is the final book in the *Friend Grief* series. Little did I know in the spring of 2006 that I would spend most of the next ten years on a new career: writing.

That was when I sat with my friend, Delle Chatman at Metropolis, the coffeehouse around the corner from our daughters' school. She was in remission from ovarian cancer for the second time and as lively and focused as ever. But as we sat there with our green teas I told her I had an idea for a book: about people grieving their friends.

As usual, she was enthusiastic and supportive. "Just do it." She waved her hand for emphasis, as if it were something easy and minor. When I reminded her I'd never written a book before, it failed to change her mind. That November, she was dead.

It was almost three years before I really got going. I'd tried several times only to fail miserably. But in the fall of 2009, I was finally able to begin to keep that promise.

Along the way, I pitched four dozen agents to no avail. One wanted me to expand the concept to include having a falling out with a friend. Another wanted me to include pets. Most liked the idea, but had no idea how to market it. Once I decided that the book would be turned in to a series of smaller books, self-publishing was the option that made the most sense. On my own, the learning curve has been steep, to put it mildly. I've been blessed to have terrific mentors along the way, along with a talented, patient production team.

The first book was published in early 2013 and now, in 2016, the series comes to an end. I've met amazing people along the way: the men and women I interviewed and the readers I've met online and in person. You'll never know how much of a difference you've made in my life.

I've been able to tie two of my books to nonprofit organizations I respect (Broadway Cares/Equity Fights AIDS and Military Outreach USA), so that the sales benefit them in some small way.

When I started on this journey, a Google search for "grieving the death of a friend" resulted in more information on grieving the death of a pet than a human friend. I like animals, but I wanted to change that. And I think I did.

Now and then I'd meet someone who would ask what I do. I'd tell them about the series and there would be a pause. "You know," they'd begin and tell me a story about a friend who died. It wasn't always as dramatic as George Davis' announcement at dinner, but some of their stories wound up in the books.

What I learned – and what I hope my readers learn – is that the bond between friends is as strong as family ties; sometimes a lot stronger. Friendships sustain us and define us throughout our lives.

The original title I considered when I began writing was *It's Not Like They're Family*, because that's the reaction many people get when they grieve a friend. Check the bereavement policy at your workplace. Some are adding "pet" as a category for paid time off, but few include "friend". So there's still work to do.

Writing this series has also brought me back to the AIDS community in a dramatic way. I did not expect or plan to get involved again. I felt like I'd served my time in the early days as a fundraiser. I was done. But I wasn't.

The second book in the series (*Friend Grief and AIDS: Thirty Years of Burying Our Friends*) triggered something in me. It brought the anger, long-suppressed, from the early days to the forefront of my life. I joined ACT UP/NY. I wrote essays and letters to the editor. I lobbied on Capitol Hill. And it sparked a desire to write a book after the *Friend Grief* series that has already received tremendous support. So, coming in 2017, *Fag Hags, Divas and Moms: The Legacy of Straight Women in the AIDS Community* will fill a gap in the existing AIDS literature. It's a daunting project that I approach with both fear and excitement.

To my readers who inspire me: I hope that you'll keep your friends close to you. Risk being embarrassed and tell them you love them. Treasure them while they're here and keep them in your heart when they're gone.

As I have said often during this journey, this is not what I thought I'd be doing at this age. But it *is* what I'm doing at this age. It's Delle's fault. I hope she's satisfied. But I have the feeling she may not be done with me yet. And that's okay. Because so far, she hasn't steered me wrong.

Acknowledgements

My deepest thanks to Paul Sullivan, Jeff Berry, George Davis, Jim Eigo, Mike Genovese, Rabbi Arthur Rosenberg and the late Pierre Jalbert for sharing their stories with me.

My beta readers: David Beckwith, Ann Mitchell, Kathy Pooler for their encouragement.

My family for their patience.

And to all those who have taken the time to tell me what my books have meant to them, you've made it all worthwhile.

References

Doka, K.J., Ed. *Disenfranchised Grief: New Directions, Challenges and Strategies for Practice*. Champaign, IL: Research Press, 2002.

Goins, Jeff. *The Clarity and Confusion of Grief,* goinswriter.com, Oct. 6, 2015.

Halkitis, Perry N. *The AIDS Generation: Stories of Survival and Resilience*. New York: Oxford University Press, 2014.

Leibenow, Mark. "Five Reasons Joe Biden's Public Grief Was Important", *Huffington Post*, Feb. 8, 2016.

Levang, Elizabeth, Ph.D. *When Men Grieve: Why Men Grieve Differently and How You Can Help Them*. Minneapolis: Fairview Press, 1998.

Morris, Jeannie. *Brian Piccolo: A Short Season*. New York: Rowman & Littlefield, 1995.

Shepard, Benjamin. *Rebel Friendships: "Outsider" Networks and Social Movements*, New York: Palgrave MacMillan, 2015.

Resources

Recommended films about men and grief:

The Concert for George

Brian's Song

50/50

Longtime Companion

How to Survive a Plague

The nonprofit organizations referenced are:

ACT UP/NY – ACTUPNY.org

Brian Piccolo Fund – BrianPiccoloFund.org

Broadway Cares/Equity Fights AIDS – BroadwayCares.org

Chapter 5 Foundation – Chapter5Foundation.com

Christopher Elliot Hallowell Fund – cehfund.org

Military Outreach USA – MilitaryOutreachUSA.org

Stop Soldier Suicide – Stopsoldiersuicide.org

Books by Victoria Noe

Friend Grief and Anger: When Your Friend Dies and No One Gives A Damn

Friend Grief and AIDS: Thirty Years of Burying Our Friends

Friend Grief and 9/11: The Forgotten Mourners

Friend Grief and the Military: Band of Friends

Friend Grief in the Workplace: More Than an Empty Cubicle

I've been a writer most of my life, but didn't admit it until 2009.

After earning a master's degree in Speech and Dramatic Art from the University of Iowa, I moved to Chicago, where I worked professionally as a stage manager, director and administrator in addition to being a founding board member of the League of Chicago Theatres. I discovered I was good at fundraising, and ventured out on my own, raising millions for arts, educational and AIDS service organizations, and later became an award-winning sales consultant of children's books. But when a concussion ended my sales career, I decided to finally keep a promise to a dying friend to write a book.

That book became a series of small books. The first three – *Friend Grief and Anger: When Your Friend Dies and No One Gives A Damn*; *Friend Grief and AIDS: Thirty Years of Burying Our Friends* and *Friend Grief and 9/11: The Forgotten Mourners* were published in 2013. *Friend Grief and the Military: Band of Friends*, was published in 2014 and earned Honorable Mention in the 2015 Chicago Writers Association Book of the Year Awards. *Friend Grief in the Workplace: More Than an Empty Cubicle* was published in 2015.

Another book, *Fag Hags, Divas and Moms: The Legacy of Straight Women in the AIDS Community,* is on track to be published in 2017.

In October, 2015, *Library Journal* named me their first SELF-e Ambassador. The first four e-books in the *Friend Grief* series are included in their Illinois and Select (national) collections. I've spoken at Writers Digest Conference, Book Expo America and their UPublishU self-publishing day.

My articles have appeared on a variety of grief and writing blogs as well as *Windy City Times, Positively Aware, A&U Magazine, Chicago Tribune* and *Huffington Post*. My essay, "Long Term Survivor" won the 2015 Christopher Hewitt Award for Creative Nonfiction.

I'm a card-carrying member of Alliance of Independent Authors (ALLi), Chicago Writers Association and ACT UP/NY (just kidding – we don't have membership cards in ACT UP).

In my copious spare time, I feed my reading habit by reviewing a wide variety of books on BroadwayWorld.com. A native St. Louisan, I'm a lifelong Cardinals fan and will gladly take on any comers in musical theatre trivia. My blog, *FriendGrief,* was named one of the top ten grief support websites in 2012.

I have no idea what's coming next, but I hope it's fun.

Join the fun by signing up for my newsletter at
www.VictoriaNoe.com

www.ingramcontent.com/pod-product-compliance
Lightning Source LLC
Chambersburg PA
CBHW052135010526
44113CB00036B/2262